400 PICKUP LINES

~~FLIRT~~ ~~LAUGH~~

CRINGE

YOUR WAY TO YOUR DREAM DATE

A note from your matchmakers!

Dear reader,

They say love is hard to find. We say you just don't have the right tools for the job... but that changes today.

In this book, you will find 400 of the finest (definitely subjective) pickup lines that are ~~not~~ guaranteed to woo the love of your life.

Many pickup lines can be adapted to suit any gender and scenario. Whether that's a randomer at a cafe or a long-term friend zone, there's an opener for you in here.

These pickup lines are satire and we definitely recommend some more than others, but remember, it's not always what you say, but how you say it.

It's the Wild West out there... good luck!!

"Behind every strong relationship was once an even stronger pickup line".

1.

Let's flip a coin... Heads, you're mine, Tails, I'm yours.

2.

I've lost my phone number. Can I have yours?

3.

What do you and cardiac arrests have in common? They both make my heart stop.

4.

Do you have a name, or can I just call you mine?

5.

Do you have a map please? It's just I keep getting lost in your eyes.

6.

I would say bless you, but by the looks of it, you've already been blessed.

7.

Are you a parking ticket? Because you've got "FINE" written all over you.

8.

Do you believe in love at first sight, or should I walk past again?

9.
Are you a campfire? Because you're hot and I always want s'more.

10.
You must be a camera because every time I look at you, I smile.

11.
Do you have a band-aid? 'Cause I've just scraped my knee falling for you.

12.
Are you a flower? 'Cause DAMN-delion.

13.

Is your name Wi-Fi by any chance?
I'm feeling a connection.

14.

Oh you must be French... 'Cause
Eiffel for you.

15.

I wish I could take you to the
movies, but they don't allow snacks.

16.

Are you a cat? Because I've never
seen someone so purrrrfect.

17.

Is your dad Muhammad Ali? Because you're a knockout!

18.

Do you work in a bank? Because you've got my interest.

19.

Want to watch Star Wars? Because Yoda one for me!

20.

You must be a banana because you're so a-peeling.

21.

Are you a combo of copper and tellurium? 'Cause you're Cu-Te!

22.

Are you a grape in disguise? Because you're looking fine as wine!

23.

Are you an alien? 'Cause you just abducted my heart.

24.

Do you like discounts? 'Cause clothes are 100% off at my house.

25.
I must be a time traveler because I can see you in my future!

26.
Are you a keyboard? Because you're exactly my type.

27.
Are you an orphanage? Because I want to give you lots of children.

28.
Is your name dictionary? Because you add meaning to my life.

29.
Are you a swimming pool? 'Cause I'm diving in head first.

30.
Do you own a bakery? Because you've got some real nice buns.

31.
You must be tired from running through my mind all day.

32.
Did you grow up in Tennessee? Because you're the only ten I see.

33.
Is this Tinder? 'Cause I've just found my dream match.

34.
Could I borrow a kiss? I promise to give it back.

35.
You're so sweet, I'm worried you will give me toothache.

36.
If I'm wrong, kiss me... I've just seen a flying pig.

37.
Are you a broom? Because you've just swept me off my feet!

38.
Please grab my arm so I can tell my friends I've been touched by an angel.

39.
Did you hurt yourself when you fell from heaven?

40.
If you were a triangle, you would most definitely be a acute one.

41.

Are you the moon? 'Cause you brighten my darkest days.

42.

Are you a vegetable? Because you look like a cutecumber.

43.

You must be an artist 'cause you just keep drawing me in.

44.

Considering nothing lasts forever, fancy being my nothing?

45.
No wonder the sky seems gray; all the blue can be found in your eyes!

46.
If only I were a transplant surgeon, I would offer you my heart.

47.
Do you know CPR? Because you've just taken my breath away!

48.
Are you a broken clock? Because time stands still when I look into your eyes.

49.

Want to get matching tattoos? 'Cause you're permanently inked on my heart.

50.

If you were a star, you'd shine the brightest.

51.

Were you born in a nuclear reactor? Because your smile is radiating.

52.

Are you a shooting star? 'Cause I wish I could be by your side tonight.

53.
If you were a flower, I'd pick you.

54.
Am I dreaming? Because you're too good to be true.

55.
Are your parents artists? Because they've created a masterpiece.

56.
Are you a wizard? Because being around you is magical.

57.
Are you a pirate? 'Cause I've just found my treasure.

58.
I'm lost; please give me the map to your heart.

59.
Are you a precious gemstone? Because you are one in a billion.

60.
Are you a book? 'Cause I want to read every chapter of your life.

61.
Do you like fairytales? 'Cause I think I've just found my happily ever after.

62.
Is your name destiny? Because meeting you feels like fate.

63.
I'm glad you aren't in my dreams because I'd never want to wake up.

64.
Sorry but you owe me a drink. I dropped mine when I looked at you.

65.
Are we at high altitude or did you just take my breath away?

66.
Do you like English breakfast? Because you're one hot-tea!

67.
If being beautiful was a crime, you'd have been arrested by now.

68.
My bed's broken. Would it be okay if I slept in yours?

69.

Your left eye must hurt because you've been looking right all day.

70.

I might not be a genie, but I promise I'll make your wishes come true.

71.

There must be a problem with my eyes; I just can't stop looking at you.

72.

My doctor has warned me that I'm missing Vitamin U in my life.

73.
Feel my shirt; it's 100% boyfriend/girlfriend material.

74.
I may not be a photographer, but I can picture you and me together.

75.
If I had to choose between you and my dog, could you tell me where the nearest kennel is?

76.
Not sure if there is an airport nearby or if it's just my heart taking off?

77.

Are you my phone charger? 'Cause I'm pretty sure I'd die without you.

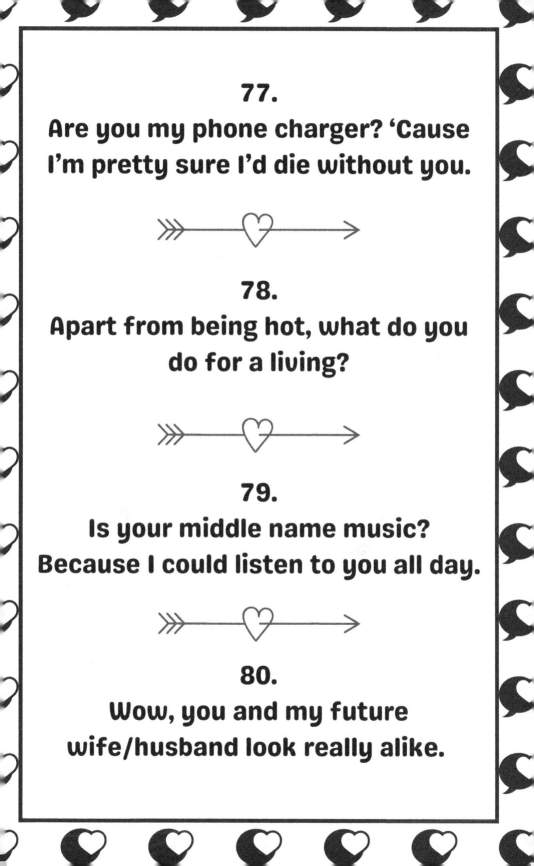

78.

Apart from being hot, what do you do for a living?

79.

Is your middle name music? Because I could listen to you all day.

80.

Wow, you and my future wife/husband look really alike.

81.

Are you God? 'Cause meeting you has answered all my prayers.

82.

Life without you is like a broken pencil... completely pointless.

83.

Are you an Amazon package? 'Cause I've been waiting for you all day.

84.

Did you go to Girl Scouts? 'Cause you've tied my heart in knots.

85.
Is it a sunny day or is that just your smile again?

86.
Right, I'm here. Now what were your other two wishes?

87.
Do you work in a cafe? Because I like you a latte.

88.
I haven't had any alcohol, I'm just intoxicated by you.

89.

If I was a penguin, I would belly slide into your DMs!

90.

Someone call the police 'cause it's surely illegal to look that good.

91.

Excuse me, I dropped something. Oh, it's just my jaw.

92.

No need for Twitter, I'm already following you. (Not recommended)

93.

Am I a snowflake? Because I've just fallen for you.

94.

Are you a pacemaker? Because you really get my heart beating.

95.

Oh no, your hand looks heavy. Should I hold it for you?

96.

How does it feel to be the most beautiful woman/man in the room?

97.

Are you a thief? Because you've just stolen my heart.

98.

My friends say I'm scared of commitment. Can you help me prove them wrong?

99.

Was your dad in the army? Because you're a rocket.

100.

Are you pizza? Because I want a pizza that.

101.
My phone seems to have a problem. It doesn't have your number.

102.
I need your name and number for insurance reasons, your beauty has blinded me.

103.
Are you my GPS? Because I'm lost without you.

104.
Has there been an earthquake or is that just you rocking my world?

105.
Are you a camel? 'Cause I'm drawn to your hump-tivating charm.

106.
Do you like what I'm wearing? It's the smile you gave me.

107.
Kissing burns five calories a minute. Wanna work out?

108.
Are you a light switch? Because you've sparked my interest.

109.

Oh maybe I'm the light switch... can you turn me on?

110.

They say you are what you eat... but I don't remember eating obsessed with you.

111.

Do your lips taste as good as they look? Just something I've been wondering.

112.

All three of my hearts would beat for you, if I were an octopus that is.

113.
Do you own dogs? 'Cause you've got me begging for your attention.

114.
Do you work at McDonalds? 'Cause you're looking McGorgeous.

115.
I can't get you out of my mind. Do you have an eraser?

116.
My feelings for you are like diarrhea; I just can't hold it in.

117.
Have you been baking again? I want a cutie pie like you!

118.
You must be a flower because the butterflies in my tummy are going crazy around you.

119.
You like my name? Wait until you hear my number.

120.
Oh, you like my surname? You can have it if you want?

121.
The sheriff is coming to arrest me. Can I hide in your bed?

122.
Can I give you a pickaxe? Because I want to make you mine.

123.
Nice to meet you. I'm chance - do I have one?

124.
You're sweeter than sweet tea on a warm spring morning.

125.

Are you made from alcohol? Because you got me feeling tipsy.

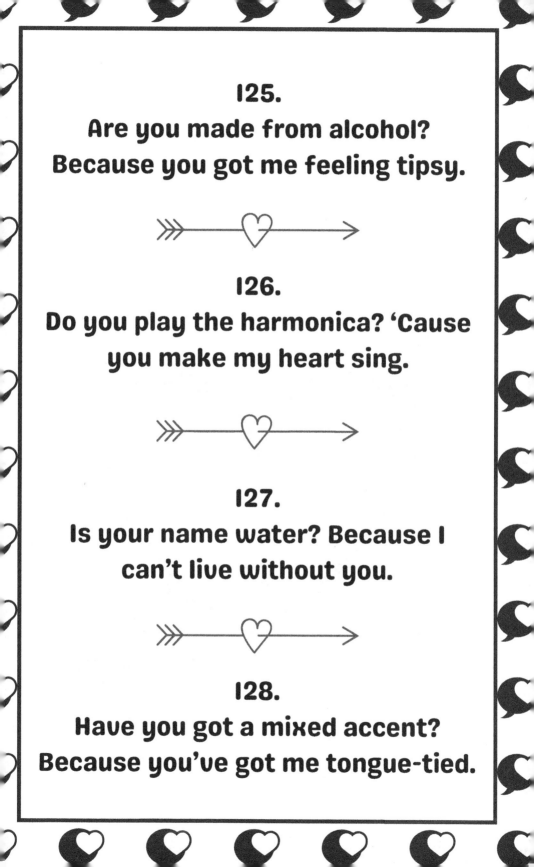

126.

Do you play the harmonica? 'Cause you make my heart sing.

127.

Is your name water? Because I can't live without you.

128.

Have you got a mixed accent? Because you've got me tongue-tied.

129.

Is your name Excel? Because I'd love to explore your sheets.

130.

Wow, it's hot in here. Oh wait - is that just you?

131.

Do you like football? 'Cause you're definitely a keeper.

132.

I like your jeans, they would look better on my bedroom floor though.

133.

Hello, just wondered if you had a minute for me to hit on you?

134.

Am I stood on ice or have you just given me cold feet?

135.

If you were a piece of fruit, you'd be a fineapple.

136.

Are you called Bluetooth? Because I'm feeling a wireless connection.

137.

You're so lip-smackingly amazing, is your name chapstick?

138.

If time was beauty, you'd be forever and a day!

139.

Are you called Ariel? Because we mermaid for each other.

140.

You're like Netflix, I could watch you for hours.

141.

Can we take a selfie? I need to prove to my friends that angels are real.

142.

I bet you attract a lot of bees. 'Cause you're sweeter than honey.

143.

If kisses were snowflakes, I'd send you a blizzard.

144.

How much do polar bears weigh? Enough to break the ice.

145.

Do you happen to have a pencil? It's just I want to erase your past and write our future.

146.

Mind if I follow you home? My parents told me to follow my dreams. (Also not recommended)

147.

If kisses were stars, you would illuminate the sky.

148.

Are you an artist? 'Cause you bring color to my life.

149.
Are you a fishing rod? 'Cause you've got me hooked from the start.

150.
Is your favorite season summer? 'Cause you make my heart melt.

151.
If I could rearrange the alphabet, I would put U and I together.

152.
Are you named after a flower? 'Cause your beauty blooms in my thoughts.

153.

Are you a candle? 'Cause you light up every room you walk into.

154.

Let's go for a run. Your pace or mine?

155.

Do you like monkeys? 'Cause your beauty is sending me bananas.

156.

If you were a book, I'd read every page from front to back.

157.

Are you a jigsaw piece? 'Cause you complete me.

158.

Are you a firework? Because you set my heart on fire.

159.

Are you a sailor? 'Cause I'm lost at sea in your eyes.

160.

You remind me of coffee 'cause you keep me up all night.

161.

Are you a compass? 'Cause you always lead my heart in the right direction.

162.

I like my women how I like my showers; hot and steamy.

163.

Are you the lottery? 'Cause meeting you feels like I've won the jackpot.

164.

Are you a key? 'Cause you've unlocked my happiness.

165.
You remind me of a telescope.
'Cause I can't take my eyes off you.

166.
You must be a volcano. 'Cause I lava
you.

167.
Are you a smart phone? 'Cause I
can't seem to put you down.

168.
Is your name Wally? 'Cause
someone like you is hard to find.

169.
Is your name gravity? 'Cause you just keep pulling me in.

170.
If beauty were a crime, you'd be served a life sentence.

171.
You're like a pair of glasses 'cause you make my feelings crystal clear.

172.
Are you on LinkedIn? 'Cause you have all the qualifications I'm looking for.

173.

If we were cats, I'd spend all 9 lives with you.

174.

You're like my iCloud 'cause my heart is in sync with you.

175.

Are you good with numbers? Because I'm ac-counting on seeing you later.

176.

Do you know what's on the menu? Me 'n u

177.

Are you called Wikipedia? 'Cause I want to discover everything about you.

178.

If I were a math problem, you'd be my solution.

179.

You love monkeys right? Because we could go swinging together.

180.

Are you an omelette? Because you've got me eggcited.

181.
If you were a browser, I'd never close your tab.

182.
You remind me of a tornado 'cause you keep sweeping me off my feet.

183.
Surely you don't have a twin 'cause you must be one-of-a-kind.

184.
Did you study photography? 'Cause you've got a picture-perfect smile.

185.

Are you Cupid? 'Cause you just shot an arrow through my heart.

186.

Are you an alarm clock? 'Cause I'd love to wake up to you.

187.

Are you a roller coaster? 'Cause I want to ride the ups and downs with you.

188.

Do you drink fizzy drinks? Because you're soda-licious.

189.
Is your name molten metal?
Because you're too hot to handle.

$$\ggg \!\!\!\!\longrightarrow \heartsuit \longrightarrow$$

190.
Are you a question mark? Because
you've got me intrigued.

$$\ggg \!\!\!\!\longrightarrow \heartsuit \longrightarrow$$

191.
We must both be human cells going
through mitosis... because we need
to multiply.

$$\ggg \!\!\!\!\longrightarrow \heartsuit \longrightarrow$$

192.
Were you any good at science?
Let's make chemistry together.

193.
Are you a mirror? 'Cause you're reflecting what I'm looking for.

194.
Are you a recipe? 'Cause I think I might be the secret ingredient.

195.
If we were at a bakers shop, you'd be the icing on my cake.

196.
Let's play a game... the winner has to date the loser.

197.

I no longer need coffee 'cause you're my daily dose of happiness.

198.

If you were a planet, you'd be the only one I'd like to explore.

199.

Are you a treasure chest? 'Cause I feel like I've struck gold.

200.

If you were a lighthouse, you'd guide me through the darkest days.

201.
You shine so bright, even the sun blushes in your presence.

202.
Why would I want to look at the sky when I can stare into your eyes?

203.
If you were a video game, you'd be Minecraft, but without the 'craft'.

204.
Are you Mariah Carey? Because all I want for Christmas is you.

205.

If the sky lost a star every time you came into my mind, the sky would be black.

206.

Are you lightning? Because you're McQueen.

207.

How am I meant to plan our wedding without your number?

208.

Oh there you are! The girl of my dreams.

209.
If your heart was a jail, I would want to be sentenced for life.

210.
How about I steal your heart and you steal mine? The perfect crime.

211.
If there was a blackout, you'd be the only thing shining.

212.
There just isn't a word invented that would describe your beauty.

213.
If you were a music award, you'd be this week's hottest single.

214.
You know what's gorgeous? The first word of my last sentence.

215.
I didn't believe in love at first sight, until I saw you.

216.
The only thing I would change about you is your last name.

217.

Got any plans for the future?
'Cause I'd like to spend it with you.

218.

There are gaps between my fingers
that were made for you.

219.

Hi, my name is [your name], but you
can just call me tomorrow.

220.

It's okay if I die because now I
know what heaven looks like.

221.

I no longer need the sun because you light up my world.

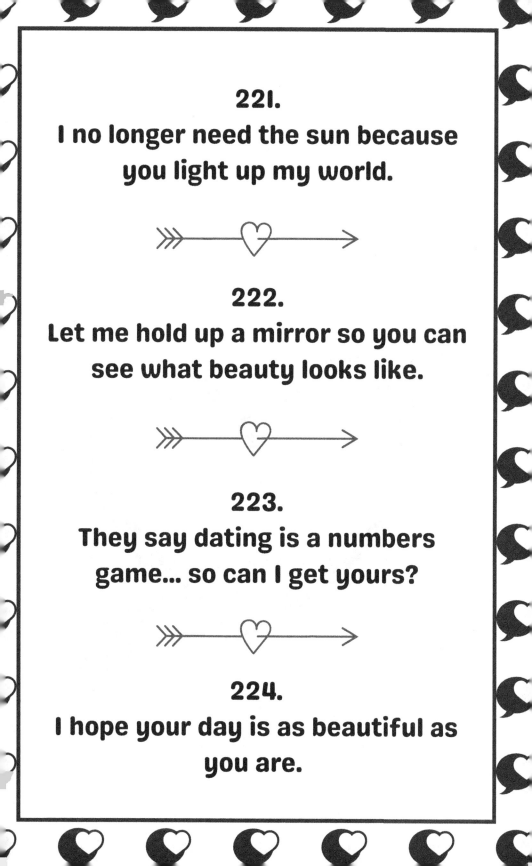

222.

Let me hold up a mirror so you can see what beauty looks like.

223.

They say dating is a numbers game... so can I get yours?

224.

I hope your day is as beautiful as you are.

225.

I don't hoard things but I'd really like to keep you forever.

226.

Happiness is supposed to start with an H, but mine starts with U.

227.

You want to know who makes my life worth living? Listen to the first word.

228.

Were the angels sad when you left heaven for earth?

229.
Are you a trip hazard? Because you make me fall hard.

230.
Excuse me, Cupid's on the phone - he wants my heart back.

231.
I'm a thief, here to steal your heart and future.

232.
Are you lost? 'Cause heaven is a long way from here.

233.

Sorry, have you seen my heart? I believe you have it.

234.

Mind if I take your photo? I need to show Santa what I want for Christmas.

235.

Is your name dinner? 'Cause I've been thinking about you all day.

236.

Did the sun just come out or was that just your smile?

237.
Are you lost? 'Cause the Miss Beautiful pageant is over there.

238.
123456789... the only number I'm missing is yours.

239.
Are you a sock too? Because we'd make a great pair.

240.
Do you remember me? I met you in my dreams last night.

241.

Do you have a broken heart? 'Cause I'll do everything I can to heal it.

242.

Wait, if you're here - who's guarding heaven?

243.

My friend thinks you're cute, but I disagree - I think you're beautiful.

244.

Please can I know what time you'll be returning to heaven?

245.

Do you have a license because you're driving me crazy.

246.

What do your beauty and the sun have in common? They both blind me.

247.

Whoever said perfection doesn't exist has never met you.

248.

Did we have a class together? I swear it was chemistry.

249.

You have something in your eye. Oh it's just a sparkle.

250.

Make sure you tie your shoelaces because I can't have you falling for anyone else.

251.

Pinch me, I must be dreaming to have met someone like you.

252.

I didn't know angels flew this low.

253.
Are you a cat? Because I've fallen fur you.

254.
Do I know you? Because I'd sure like to.

255.
Do you mind giving me a tour through your mind?

256.
Do you sell tickets to your heart? 'Cause I'd like one please.

257.
I'm not an electrician but I can light up your day.

258.
Do you have a New Year's resolution? 'Cause you are mine.

259.
You're so good looking I forgot my pickup line.

260.
Do you like raisins? No? How about a date?

261.

You don't need that cupcake, you're sweet enough as it is.

262.

Don't leave, you've forgot something - me!

263.

Your only flaw is your lips 'cause they're not touching mine.

264.

Are you an astronaut? 'Cause your body is out of this world.

265.

You must be a magnet 'cause I'm so drawn to your beauty.

266.

I'm glad I'm an organ donor because I want to give you my heart.

267.

Am I dancing with the devil? 'Cause you're fire as hell.

268.

Are you a kidnapper? 'Cause girl, you've just abducted my heart.

269.

Surely you've lost your driving license from driving guys crazy.

270.

Move away from the bar, you're so hot you'll melt the ice.

271.

The language of love is kissing. Want to have a conversation?

272.

If I had $1 every time I thought of you, I'd only have $1... because I'm always thinking of you.

273.
You're the reason men still believe in love.

274.
You're almost perfect, except for one thing - you're not mine.

275.
God was definitely showing off when he made you.

276.
Do you have a name? If not, I could maybe call you later.

277.

I like my coffee how I like my women/men... single.

278.

Your lips look like they need company. Want to meet mine?

279.

You look cold. Want to use me as a blanket?

280.

Your dad must be a preacher 'cause you're my biggest blessing.

281.
Tell me a secret - where do you hide your wings?

282.
My lips aren't gonna kiss themselves. Can you help?

283.
Erm hello, may I flirt with you?

284.
I won't use a pickup line if you let me buy you a drink.

285.

I don't know you but I think I'm already in love.

286.

You like Excel too? Looks like we're both good in the sheets then.

287.

Want the key to my heart? It's pretty easy to unlock.

288.

My lips are hurting. Can you kiss them better?

289.

I've lost my teddy. Can you sleep with me instead?

290.

I bet we'd look great on top of a wedding cake together.

291.

Have I got a rash or am I just itching to make you mine?

292.

Your eyes are like a computer screen, I could stare at them all day long.

293.
Is your birthday October 10th?
'Cause you're 10/10.

294.
Know any real estate? I'm trying to
make a move here.

295.
Good job I have my library card
'cause I'm checking you out.

296.
I've been told to follow my dreams
so can I have your Instagram?

297.

Shall we talk about climate change? I need to break the ice here.

298.

You're like my wisdom tooth, I need to take you out asap.

299.

You look like you could do with some Vitamin Me.

300.

I think you're really grate, sorry if that sounds cheesy.

301.

I've got you some new trainers 'cause you've been running through my mind all day.

302.

Are you dunkin? 'Cause I donut want to spend time without you.

303.

On a scale of one to America, how free are you tonight?

304.

Roses are red, violets are blue, I've just pulled a muscle, now can I pull you?

305.
Ouch, are you fresh from the oven? 'Cause you're too hot to handle.

306.
Roses are red, violets are blue... we're meant to be together and you know it's true.

307.
I was feeling off today, but you've turned me on.

308.
Quick - Stop, drop and roll! You're on fire!!

309.

Out of all the potatoes, you'd be a sweet one.

310.

Are you a model? No? Oh! Why did you quit?

311.

Fancy some wine to go with this cheesy pick up line?

312.

Finally, the cutie pie I ordered has arrived!

313.
I won't break your hurt, I promise - I'll only steal it.

314.
Are you the Mona Lisa? 'Cause you're a work of art.

315.
I don't know your name but I bet it's as gorgeous as you are.

316.
Are you a broken traffic light? Because you're not giving me mixed signals.

317.
I'm not an organ donor but I'll certainly give you my heart.

318.
Are you Instagram? Because I'm addicted to you.

319.
I can see you're beautiful but what else should I know about you?

320.
If I'm the prince, will you be my Tinderella?

321.

Have we met before? You look a lot like the love of my life.

322.

So, I'm cute and you're pretty. Wanna be pretty cute together?

323.

Know what you'd look amazing in? My arms.

324.

Are your parents musicians? Because they produced the hottest single of all time.

325.

When I text you hello, what number should I text?

326.

So what emoji do you want next to your name in my phone?

327.

I believe your number will be a lot safer in my phone than your head.

328.

If you were a garden accessory, you'd be a barbecute.

329.

You have nice arms. Can I see how they feel wrapped around me?

330.

I had a good pickup line but you've left me speechless.

331.

Are you a math equation? 'Cause you got me stumped.

332.

You should walk round with a hazard sign because that smile is dangerous.

333.

When you get rich and older, will you be my cougar?

334.

Wanna play connect the dots but with our bodies?

335.

You must be from Jamaica 'cause you Jamaican me crazy!

336.

Do you live in a zoo? 'Cause I wanna get up close and personal to you!

337.

If you were a tattoo, you'd be a FINE line.

338.

It's cold in here. Want to keep warm together?

339.

Sorry, were you talking to me? No? Do you want to?

340.

Excuse me, do you have an extra heart? Mine just got stolen.

341.

Are we playing hide and seek? Girls like you are hard to find.

342.

I don't like your surname. Do you want mine instead?

343.

I have a knife and fork, all I need now is a little spoon.

344.

I hope you know CPR because you just made my heart stop.

345.

I bet my number is better than yours. Want to hear it?

346.

Fancy a game of truth or date? I'll go first, date?

347.

Are you a magician? Because when I look at you, everyone else seems to disappear.

348.

I bet the stars are jealous of the sparkle in your eyes.

349.

Nice to meet you; I'm Mr Right. Heard you were after me?

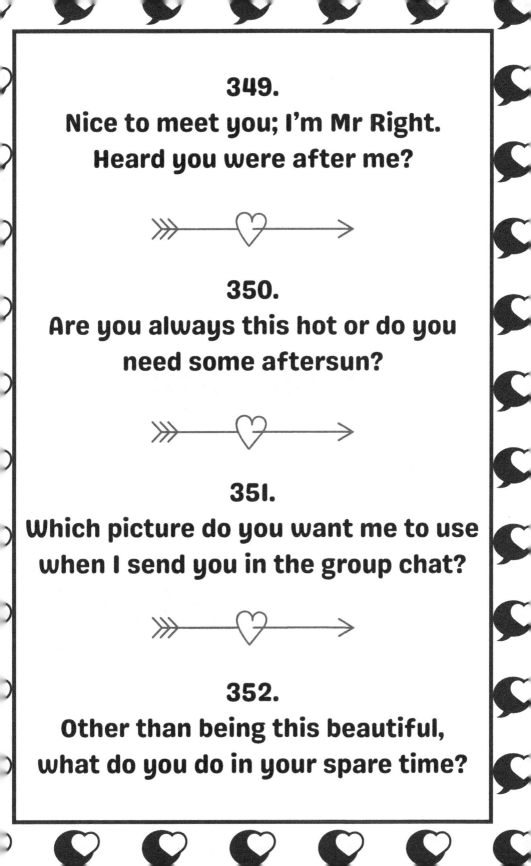

350.

Are you always this hot or do you need some aftersun?

351.

Which picture do you want me to use when I send you in the group chat?

352.

Other than being this beautiful, what do you do in your spare time?

353.

Your parents were really showing off when they made you.

354.

Are you called Google? Because you're everything I've been searching for.

355.

Titanic? Sorry, that's just my icebreaker.

356.

I would flirt, but instead I'll seduce you with my awkwardness.

357.

I do normally go for 8s but this time I'll settle for a 10.

358.

Are you from Mexico? I want to make you my Bae-ritto.

359.

You'll never know the amount of left swipes it took to get to you.

360.

I'm not too sure how this all works. Are we married now?

361.
You owe me new shoes, 'cause I tripped whilst looking at you.

362.
Do you like fruit? I think we'd be a great pear.

363.
Do you eat bagels? 'Cause you're my bae goals.

364.
Are you a basketball 3-pointer? Because you're definitely worth a shot.

365.
Even if there was no gravity, I'd still fall for you.

366.
Can you catch butterflies? There's a huge one in my stomach right now.

367.
I actually swiped for the dog, but now I'm staying for the human.

368.
I'd sacrifice my morning cereal to spoon you instead.

369.

How have you managed to draw my attention without a pen?

370.

Saw you like food? I know a couple of things you could taste.

371.

Can you add me to your "to-do" list please?

372.

When I make you breakfast in the morning, what do you fancy?

373.

If I said you have a great body, would you hold it against me?

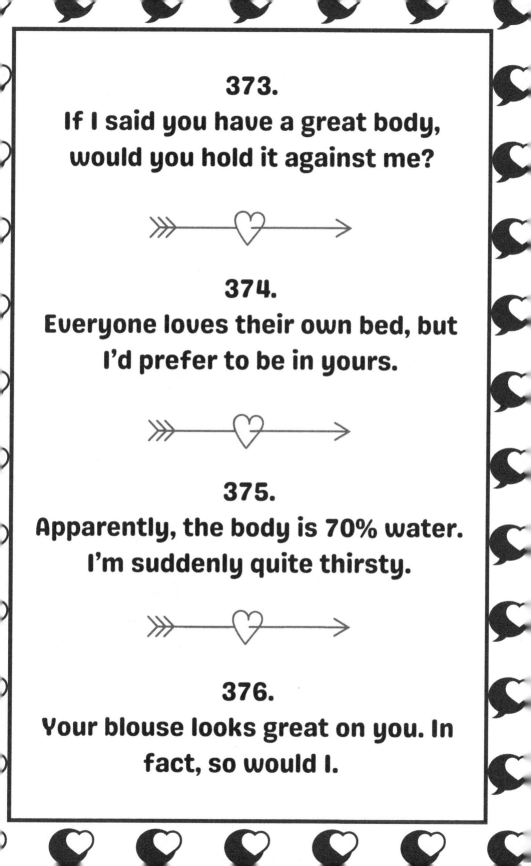

374.

Everyone loves their own bed, but I'd prefer to be in yours.

375.

Apparently, the body is 70% water. I'm suddenly quite thirsty.

376.

Your blouse looks great on you. In fact, so would I.

377.
You look so good in clothes, bet you look even better without them.

378.
I'm really just not feeling myself today. Can I feel you instead?

379.
You like sleeping? Same, maybe we should do it together one day.

380.
You get to choose this one, my place or yours?

381.

At what age did you discover you were so beautiful?

382.

I'm new to all of this. I'm guessing we kiss now?

383.

Shall I tell you my life story now or do we wait until the first date?

384.

We're a better match than peanut butter and jelly.

385.

So then, how long have you been working for Vogue?

386.

I'm so crazy in love, that I'm starting to think I'm Beyonce.

387.

Are you any good at solving math problems? What's you plus me?

388.

Did it hurt when you fell from the vending machine? Because you're a snack.

389.

Are you on the run? Surely it's illegal to look that amazing.

390.

Will I get a tan next to you? 'Cause you're hotter than the sun.

391.

Were you born a beaver? Because daaaaaaaaam!

392.

Got a shovel? 'Cause I'm digging you.

393.
Can you help me get on Santa's naughty list this year?

394.
You look like a glass of water and damn, I'm parched.

395.
Did your car battery die? I'd love to jump you.

396.
I love your T-shirt. Can I try it on tomorrow morning?

397.

Nice trousers you've got there. Can I talk you out of them?

398.

Is your body a map? 'Cause I'm ready to go traveling.

399.

Wow, your belt looks a bit tight. Want me to loosen it for you?

400.

You look like you enjoy eating bacon. Wanna strip?